AF597950

Sacred Heart of Jesus

Devotion to
Jesus' Heart
for Children

Sacred Heart of JESUS

Written by Patrick O'Hearn

Illustrated by Adalee Hude

Foreword by
Raymond Leo Cardinal Burke

SOPHIA INSTITUTE PRESS
Manchester, New Hampshire

Cover design by Emma Helstrom in collaboration with Perceptions Studio.

Interior design by Perceptions Studio.

Cover and interior artwork by Adalee Hude.

Sophia Institute Press
Box 5284, Manchester, NH 03108
1-800-888-9344
www.SophiaInstitute.com

Sophia Institute Press® is a registered trademark of Sophia Institute.

hardcover ISBN 979-8-88911-388-1
ebook ISBN 979-8-88911-389-8

Library of Congress Control Number: 2025938581

First printing

This book is lovingly dedicated to Eveyln.
–P. O.

This book is lovingly dedicated to Margot.
–A. H.

Contents

Foreword

I was born in 1948 to parents who loved the Catholic Church with a love that seemed very much like the love they offered to their children. To put it another way, when I was a child, the Church seemed like family. Parish priests were another kind of father. Religious sisters were another kind of mother. The love and teaching they gave to me felt like an expansion of my father and mother's parenthood. The years of my early youth in the late 1940s and into the 1950s were filled with the richness of our Catholic traditions, which always seemed to be like family traditions.

One of those traditions was the enthronement of an image of the Sacred Heart of Jesus in an important and visible place in my family's home. It seemed to me, as a child, that this enthronement made Jesus the most important member of our family. We understood that He is Our Savior, the King of Heaven and Earth, but now we could see Him watching over us as a father and brother, as the King of our hearts. The image of His Sacred Heart, so prominently placed in our home, was a sign of His great and wonderful love for us. The image would stay with me throughout the day. I could see that image of His Sacred Heart when I left the house to go to school or to the church to adore and receive His Real Presence in the Holy Eucharist. The Sacred Heart was the permanent guest in our home, as much as He was also the permanent guest of our hearts through the sevenfold gift of the Holy Spirit. In this way, my devotion to the Sacred Heart of Jesus became ever more strongly linked to my Eucharistic devotion.

Devotion to the Sacred Heart of Jesus both flows from Eucharistic devotion and, at the same time, increases its fervor. Devotion to the Sacred Heart of Jesus is devotion to the mystery of Divine Love

Incarnate, Jesus Christ, the mystery that finds the fullness of its expression in the Eucharistic Sacrifice. So I urge you to develop a strong devotion to the Sacred Heart of Jesus, as a most effective means of living in the Presence of our Eucharistic Lord at all times, of preparing for participation in the Holy Mass, and of bringing the Holy Eucharist into every aspect of your life. Devotion to the Sacred Heart of Jesus will help you to think, speak, and act with Jesus in meeting the daily challenges of life. The purity of love of the Heart of Jesus will discipline and purify your desires and affections, so that Jesus may truly reign in your heart for the salvation of the world.

Mr. Patrick O'Hearn's book on the Sacred Heart of Jesus is an excellent companion to help your devotion to the Sacred Heart of Jesus to grow into a deep and abiding love for God and for your neighbor. It will help you to place your heart, one with the Immaculate Heart of Mary, the Mother of Jesus, always more completely in the Sacred Heart of Jesus. In His Sacred Heart, you will find the joy and peace for which we all long now and, one day, will know perfectly in Heaven.

—Raymond Leo Cardinal Burke

Introduction

There are many devotions in the Catholic Church, but there is none so powerful as consoling the Sacred Heart of Jesus. You might have seen images of the Sacred Heart of Jesus with thorns and flames. A tiny cross appears above the Sacred Heart. The flames represent Jesus' burning love for us.

Jesus told St. Margaret Mary Alacoque that He would grant the following twelve promises to those who honor His Sacred Heart:

1. I will give them all the graces necessary in their state of life.
2. I will establish peace in their homes.
3. I will comfort them in all their afflictions.
4. I will be their secure refuge during life, and above all, in death.
5. I will bestow abundant blessings upon all their undertakings.
6. Sinners will find in my Heart the source and infinite ocean of mercy.
7. Lukewarm souls shall become fervent.
8. Fervent souls shall quickly mount to high perfection.
9. I will bless every place in which an image of my Heart is exposed and honored.
10. I will give to priests the gift of touching the most hardened hearts.
11. Those who shall promote this devotion shall have their names written in my Heart.

12. I promise you in the excessive mercy of my Heart that my all-powerful love will grant to all those who receive Holy Communion on the First Fridays in nine consecutive months the grace of final perseverance; they shall not die in my disgrace, nor without receiving their sacraments. My divine Heart shall be their safe refuge in this last moment.

To console Jesus' Heart is the greatest thing we can do in this life. In this book, you will find Scripture references to the Sacred Heart of Jesus, accompanied by beautiful images, reflections, and prayers. Jesus' words to the children include private revelations given to St. Margaret Mary, St. Gertrude, and St. Faustina along with the author's inspiration. You will also see images of nine symbolic flowers that relate to Jesus' love and His Passion: (1) the red rose, (2) the pomegranate, (3) the red carnation, (4) the dogwood, (5) the myrtle, (6) the thistle, (7) the red poppy, (8) the passionflower, and (9) the hyssop.

You may read *Sacred Heart of Jesus* in one sitting or read one reflection on the first Friday of each month for nine months, according to Our Lord's twelfth promise. May all who read this book, both young and old, be inspired to love Jesus' Sacred Heart with the greatest devotion. Those who practice this powerful devotion of consoling and honoring Jesus' Sacred Heart, especially by receiving Holy Communion on the First Fridays of nine consecutive months, will have the "grace of final perseverance."

Most Sacred Heart of Jesus, have mercy on us!

Sacred Heart of Jesus

First Friday (I)

The Tiny Heart of Jesus

And the angel said to her, "Do not be afraid, Mary, for you have found favor with God. And behold, you will conceive in your womb and bear a son, and you shall call his name Jesus. He will be great, and will be called the Son of the Most High; and the Lord God will give to him the throne of his father David, and he will reign over the house of Jacob for ever; and of his kingdom there will be no end."

—Luke 1:30–33

Jesus

My child, I came into this world just for you. I left my throne in Heaven for a different throne. My throne on earth was my Mother's womb. It was there that my tiny Sacred Heart was being formed. It was there that my tiny Sacred Heart began to beat for you. With every beat, I thought about you. And yet, few people love me after all that I have done. If it were necessary to save you again, I would suffer everything for you alone. Please offer an Our Father to console my Sacred Heart.

Our Father

English & Latin

Our Father, who art in Heaven, hallowed be Thy name; Thy kingdom come; Thy will be done, on earth as it is in Heaven. Give us this day our daily bread, and forgive us our trespasses as we forgive those who trespass against us. And lead us not into temptation, but deliver us from evil. Amen.

Pater noster, qui es in caelis, sanctificétur nomen tuum; advéniat regnum tuum; fiat volúntas tua, sicut in caelo et in terra. Panem nostrum quotidiánum da nobis hódie, et dimítte nobis débita nostra, sicut et nos dimíttimus debitóribus nostris. Et ne nos indúcas in tentatiónem sed líbera nos a malo. Amen.

Prayer

O Sacred Heart of Jesus, You who hold the world in Your hands, You came to dwell in the womb of the Blessed Mother. Help me to live for You alone. Help my heart to beat for Your Heart. Help me to love as You do. I ask this in Your Holy Name. Amen.

First Friday (II)

The Infant Heart of Jesus

When the angels went away from them into heaven, the shepherds said to one another, "Let us go over to Bethlehem and see this thing that has happened, which the Lord has made known to us." And they went with haste, and found Mary and Joseph, and the babe lying in a manger. And when they saw it they made known the saying which had been told them concerning this child; and all who heard it wondered at what the shepherds told them. But Mary kept all these things, pondering them in her heart. And the shepherds returned, glorifying and praising God for all they had heard and seen, as it had been told them.

—Luke 2:15–20

Jesus

My child, I was born in a cold cave for you. My infant Heart was so in love with you. The first eyes I saw were my mother Mary's and then my father Joseph's. They loved me with the greatest love. My Mother put my Heart next to her Immaculate Heart. Our hearts beat for one another. Like her, I kept all these things in my Sacred Heart. I never wanted to leave my Mother's arms. So many hearts are cold toward my love. Please offer an Our Father to console my Sacred Heart.

Our Father

English & Latin

Our Father, who art in Heaven, hallowed be Thy name; Thy kingdom come; Thy will be done, on earth as it is in Heaven. Give us this day our daily bread, and forgive us our trespasses as we forgive those who trespass against us. And lead us not into temptation, but deliver us from evil. Amen.

Pater noster, qui es in caelis, sanctificétur nomen tuum; advéniat regnum tuum; fiat volúntas tua, sicut in caelo et in terra. Panem nostrum quotidiánum da nobis hódie, et dimítte nobis débita nostra, sicut et nos dimíttimus debitóribus nostris. Et ne nos indúcas in tentatiónem sed líbera nos a malo. Amen.

Prayer

O Sacred Heart of Jesus, You who became a little baby, help me to become small like You. You were poor; help me not to love riches. Help me to love Mary and St. Joseph as You do. Help me to become humble and simple like the shepherds. I ask this in Your Holy Name. Amen.

First Friday (III)

The Hidden Heart of Jesus

And he went down with them and came to Nazareth, and was obedient to them; and his mother kept all these things in her heart. And Jesus increased in wisdom and in stature, and in favor with God and man.

—Luke 2:51–52

Jesus

My child, I spent thirty years of my life hidden from the world. I obeyed my parents, Joseph and Mary, to teach you to be obedient. Peace reigned in our humble home in Nazareth. Our home was poor, but our love was rich. My Sacred Heart was so tenderly loved by my parents. No one loved my Heart more than my parents. In many homes today, my Sacred Heart is forgotten. Few families have an image of my Sacred Heart. Few families truly love me. Please offer an Our Father to console my Sacred Heart.

Our Father

English & Latin

Our Father, who art in Heaven, hallowed be Thy name; Thy kingdom come; Thy will be done, on earth as it is in Heaven. Give us this day our daily bread, and forgive us our trespasses as we forgive those who trespass against us. And lead us not into temptation, but deliver us from evil. Amen.

Pater noster, qui es in caelis, sanctificétur nomen tuum; advéniat regnum tuum; fiat volúntas tua, sicut in caelo et in terra. Panem nostrum quotidiánum da nobis hódie, et dimítte nobis débita nostra, sicut et nos dimíttimus debitóribus nostris. Et ne nos indúcas in tentatiónem sed líbera nos a malo. Amen.

Prayer

O Sacred Heart of Jesus, You who loved and obeyed your parents, Joseph and Mary, help me always to obey my father and my mother. Help me to love Your Heart as Joseph and Mary did and to prefer being hidden rather than being praised by the world. I ask this in Your Holy Name. Amen.

First Friday (IV)

The Humble Heart of Jesus

Come to me, all who labor and are heavy laden,
and I will give you rest. Take my yoke upon you,
and learn from me; for I am gentle and lowly
in heart, and you will find rest for your souls.
For my yoke is easy, and my burden is light.

—Matthew 11:28–30

Jesus

My child, look at my humble Heart. Now give me your heart. When you are tired and burdened, come and rest on my Heart. When you are sad and hopeless, come and rest on my Heart. So often, I am the last person you seek when you are going through trials. How sad. I want to be first in your life. My humble Heart only wants to help you. I want to take away your prideful heart and give you my humble Heart. Please offer an Our Father to console my Sacred Heart.

Our Father

English & Latin

Our Father, who art in Heaven, hallowed be Thy name; Thy kingdom come; Thy will be done, on earth as it is in Heaven. Give us this day our daily bread, and forgive us our trespasses as we forgive those who trespass against us. And lead us not into temptation, but deliver us from evil. Amen.

Pater noster, qui es in caelis, sanctificétur nomen tuum; advéniat regnum tuum; fiat volúntas tua, sicut in caelo et in terra. Panem nostrum quotidiánum da nobis hódie, et dimítte nobis débita nostra, sicut et nos dimíttimus debitóribus nostris. Et ne nos indúcas in tentatiónem sed líbera nos a malo. Amen.

Prayer

O Sacred Heart of Jesus, You who had nowhere to rest Your Head when You walked this earth, draw my heart to Yours. When I am tired and worried, refresh me and teach me how to be gentle and humble like Your Sacred Heart. I ask this in Your Holy Name. Amen.

First Friday (V)

The Childlike Heart of Jesus

Then children were brought to him that he might lay his hands on them and pray. The disciples rebuked the people; but Jesus said, "Let the children come to me, and do not hinder them; for to such belongs the kingdom of heaven." And he laid his hands on them and went away.

—Matthew 19:13–15

Jesus

My child, my Sacred Heart is waiting for you. I long to hold you in my arms. I long to press your heart next to my Sacred Heart. As the years go by and you grow older, you might think that you no longer need me. You might think that I no longer care about you. This would sadden me greatly. My loving Heart, the Heart of your best Friend, is listening to you. Your love for me must always remain childlike. Hide nothing from me. Please offer an Our Father to console my Sacred Heart.

Our Father

English & Latin

Our Father, who art in Heaven, hallowed be Thy name; Thy kingdom come; Thy will be done, on earth as it is in Heaven. Give us this day our daily bread, and forgive us our trespasses as we forgive those who trespass against us. And lead us not into temptation, but deliver us from evil. Amen.

Pater noster, qui es in caelis, sanctificétur nomen tuum; advéniat regnum tuum; fiat volúntas tua, sicut in caelo et in terra. Panem nostrum quotidiánum da nobis hódie, et dimítte nobis débita nostra, sicut et nos dimíttimus debitóribus nostris. Et ne nos indúcas in tentatiónem sed líbera nos a malo. Amen.

Prayer

O Sacred Heart of Jesus, You who welcomed all children, help me always to have a childlike trust and faith in You. Hold me in Your arms, especially when I am afraid. Keep me always close to Your Sacred Heart and let me never be separated from You. I ask this in Your Holy Name. Amen.

First Friday (VI)

The Betrayed Heart of Jesus

When Jesus had thus spoken, he was troubled in spirit, and testified, "Truly, truly, I say to you, one of you will betray me." The disciples looked at one another, uncertain of whom he spoke. One of his disciples, whom Jesus loved, was lying close to the breast of Jesus; so Simon Peter beckoned to him and said, "Tell us who it is of whom he speaks." So lying thus, close to the breast of Jesus, he said to him, "Lord, who is it?"

—John 13:21-25

Jesus

My child, my Sacred Heart was in so much pain after my friend and apostle Judas betrayed me. He sold me for thirty pieces of silver. Was I not worth more to him? Thankfully, my beloved apostle John was resting near my Sacred Heart. He loved me dearly. How I long for you to rest near my Sacred Heart. How I long for you to give me your love for those who continue to hurt me. Please offer an Our Father to console my Sacred Heart.

Our Father

English & Latin

Our Father, who art in Heaven, hallowed be Thy name; Thy kingdom come; Thy will be done, on earth as it is in Heaven. Give us this day our daily bread, and forgive us our trespasses as we forgive those who trespass against us. And lead us not into temptation, but deliver us from evil. Amen.

Pater noster, qui es in caelis, sanctificétur nomen tuum; advéniat regnum tuum; fiat volúntas tua, sicut in caelo et in terra. Panem nostrum quotidiánum da nobis hódie, et dimítte nobis débita nostra, sicut et nos dimíttimus debitóribus nostris. Et ne nos indúcas in tentatiónem sed líbera nos a malo. Amen.

Prayer

O Sacred Heart of Jesus, You who were betrayed by Judas, help me always to stay faithful to You. Forgive me when I betray You by my coldness and my sins. Help me to love You as Your beloved apostle John did, by staying near Your Heart. I ask this in Your Holy Name. Amen.

First Friday (VII)

The Agonizing Heart of Jesus

Then Jesus went with them to a place called Gethsemane, and he said to his disciples, "Sit here, while I go yonder and pray." And taking with him Peter and the two sons of Zebedee, he began to be sorrowful and troubled. Then he said to them, "My soul is very sorrowful, even to death; remain here, and watch with me." And going a little farther he fell on his face and prayed, "My Father, if it be possible, let this cup pass from me; nevertheless, not as I will, but as thou wilt."

—Matthew 26:36–39

Jesus

My child, my Sacred Heart was in so much agony and sadness in the Garden of Gethsemane. My sweat became drops of blood. In that moment, I saw every sin until the end of time. I saw all the pain and suffering I would endure for you. And I saw all of the souls to whom my suffering and death would mean nothing. Even the apostles who stayed with me fell asleep. And later, most of my apostles abandoned me. Make me some return for my love. Please offer an Our Father to console my Sacred Heart.

Our Father

English & Latin

Our Father, who art in Heaven, hallowed be Thy name; Thy kingdom come; Thy will be done, on earth as it is in Heaven. Give us this day our daily bread, and forgive us our trespasses as we forgive those who trespass against us. And lead us not into temptation, but deliver us from evil. Amen.

Pater noster, qui es in caelis, sanctificétur nomen tuum; advéniat regnum tuum; fiat volúntas tua, sicut in caelo et in terra. Panem nostrum quotidiánum da nobis hódie, et dimítte nobis débita nostra, sicut et nos dimíttimus debitóribus nostris. Et ne nos indúcas in tentatiónem sed líbera nos a malo. Amen.

Prayer

O Sacred Heart of Jesus, You who were abandoned by most of Your apostles, help me to be strong when suffering comes. Forgive me for the times when I have abandoned You. Help me always to remain near Your Heart when I am tempted to leave You. I ask this in Your Holy Name. Amen.

First Friday (VIII)

The Pierced Heart of Jesus

But one of the soldiers pierced his side with a spear, and at once there came out blood and water. He who saw it has borne witness—his testimony is true, and he knows that he tells the truth—that you also may believe. For these things took place that the scripture might be fulfilled, "Not a bone of him shall be broken." And again another scripture says, "They shall look on him whom they have pierced."

—John 19:34–37

Jesus

My child, my Sacred Heart was pierced for you on the Cross. Blood and water poured forth from it as a fountain of mercy. I gave every drop of blood for you and for all sinners, so that you might have eternal life. Come, then, with trust to draw graces from this fountain. I never reject a contrite heart. Look at my Sacred Heart on the Cross with great love for those who do not believe, do not adore, do not hope, and do not love me. Please offer an Our Father to console my Sacred Heart.

Our Father

English & Latin

Our Father, who art in Heaven, hallowed be Thy name; Thy kingdom come; Thy will be done, on earth as it is in Heaven. Give us this day our daily bread, and forgive us our trespasses as we forgive those who trespass against us. And lead us not into temptation, but deliver us from evil. Amen.

Pater noster, qui es in caelis, sanctificétur nomen tuum; advéniat regnum tuum; fiat volúntas tua, sicut in caelo et in terra. Panem nostrum quotidiánum da nobis hódie, et dimítte nobis débita nostra, sicut et nos dimíttimus debitóribus nostris. Et ne nos indúcas in tentatiónem sed líbera nos a malo. Amen.

Prayer

O Sacred Heart of Jesus, You who were pierced by a spear, help me always to stand by You. Thank You for dying for me. Wash me with Your blood and Your water, so that I might be pure. Hide me under the shadow of Your Cross from my enemies. I ask this in Your Holy Name. Amen.

First Friday (IX)

The Eucharistic Heart of Jesus

When he was at table with them, he took the bread and blessed, and broke it, and gave it to them. And their eyes were opened and they recognized him; and he vanished out of their sight. They said to each other, "Did not our hearts burn within us while he talked to us on the road, while he opened to us the scriptures?" And they rose that same hour and returned to Jerusalem; and they found the eleven gathered together and those who were with them, who said, "The Lord has risen indeed, and has appeared to Simon!" Then they told what had happened on the road, and how he was known to them in the breaking of the bread.

—Luke 24:30–35

Jesus

My child, behold this Heart, which has loved you so much and has given you everything. And in return, I receive nothing but ingratitude from most people by their coldness and irreverence for me in the Blessed Sacrament, the Sacrament of Love. Few people believe that I am truly present in the Holy Eucharist. This breaks my Heart. My delight is to be with you. Remember that I am with you always, even to the end of the world. And I wish to be frequently received in the Holy Eucharist. Please offer an Our Father to console my Sacred Heart.

Our Father

English & Latin

Our Father, who art in Heaven, hallowed be Thy name; Thy kingdom come; Thy will be done, on earth as it is in Heaven. Give us this day our daily bread, and forgive us our trespasses as we forgive those who trespass against us. And lead us not into temptation, but deliver us from evil. Amen.

Pater noster, qui es in caelis, sanctificétur nomen tuum; advéniat regnum tuum; fiat volúntas tua, sicut in caelo et in terra. Panem nostrum quotidiánum da nobis hódie, et dimítte nobis débita nostra, sicut et nos dimíttimus debitóribus nostris. Et ne nos indúcas in tentatiónem sed líbera nos a malo. Amen.

Prayer

O Sacred Heart of Jesus, You who are truly present in the Holy Eucharist, draw my heart to Yours. Thank You for giving me Your Body and Your Blood. Grant me the grace of final perseverance so that I may always stay faithful to You until death. I ask this in Your Holy Name. Amen.

Litany of the Sacred Heart of Jesus

Lord, have mercy on us.
Christ, have mercy on us.
Lord, have mercy on us. Christ, hear us.
Christ, graciously hear us.
God the Father of Heaven, *have mercy on us.*
God the Son, Redeemer of the world, *have mercy on us.*
God the Holy Spirit, *have mercy on us.*
Holy Trinity, one God, *have mercy on us.*

Heart of Jesus, Son of the Eternal Father, *have mercy on us.*
Heart of Jesus, formed by the Holy Spirit in the womb of the Virgin Mother, *have mercy on us.*
Heart of Jesus, substantially united to the word of God, *have mercy on us.*
Heart of Jesus, of Infinite Majesty, *have mercy on us.*
Heart of Jesus, Holy Temple of God, *have mercy on us.*

Heart of Jesus, Tabernacle of the Most High,
have mercy on us.
Heart of Jesus, House of God and Gate of Heaven,
have mercy on us.
Heart of Jesus, burning furnace of charity, *have mercy on us.*
Heart of Jesus, abode of justice and love, *have mercy on us.*
Heart of Jesus, full of goodness and love, *have mercy on us.*
Heart of Jesus, abyss of all virtue, *have mercy on us.*
Heart of Jesus, most worthy of all praise, *have mercy on us.*
Heart of Jesus, king and center of all hearts, *have mercy on us.*
Heart of Jesus, treasure-house of wisdom and knowledge,
have mercy on us.
Heart of Jesus, in whom dwells the fullness of divinity,
have mercy on us.
Heart of Jesus, in whom the Father is well pleased,
have mercy on us.
Heart of Jesus, from whose fullness we have all received,
have mercy on us.
Heart of Jesus, desire of the everlasting hills, *have mercy on us.*
Heart of Jesus, patient and full of mercy, *have mercy on us.*
Heart of Jesus, generous to all who turn to You, *have mercy on us.*
Heart of Jesus, fountain of life and holiness, *have mercy on us.*
Heart of Jesus, propitiation for our sins, *have mercy on us.*
Heart of Jesus, overwhelmed with insults, *have mercy on us.*
Heart of Jesus, bruised for our offenses, *have mercy on us.*

Heart of Jesus, obedient unto death, *have mercy on us.*
Heart of Jesus, pierced by a lance, *have mercy on us.*
Heart of Jesus, source of all consolation, *have mercy on us.*
Heart of Jesus, our life and resurrection, *have mercy on us.*
Heart of Jesus, our peace and reconciliation, *have mercy on us.*
Heart of Jesus, victim for our sins, *have mercy on us.*
Heart of Jesus, salvation of those who trust in You, *have mercy on us.*
Heart of Jesus, hope of all who die in You, *have mercy on us.*
Heart of Jesus, delight of all the saints, *have mercy on us.*

Lamb of God, who takes away the sins of the world,
spare us, O Lord.
Lamb of God, who takes away the sins of the world,
graciously hear us, O Lord.
Lamb of God, who takes away the sins of the world,
have mercy on us.

Jesus, meek and humble of heart, *make our hearts like unto Thine.*

Let us pray.
Almighty and eternal God, look upon the Heart of Thy Most Beloved Son and upon the praises and satisfaction which He offers Thee in the name of sinners; and to those who implore Thy mercy, in Thy great goodness, grant forgiveness in the name of the same Jesus Christ, Thy Son, who lives and reigns with Thee forever and ever. Amen.

Traditional Prayers for Children

Sign of the Cross

In the Name of the Father, and of the Son, and of the Holy Spirit. Amen.

In Nómine Patris, et Fílii, et Spíritus Sancti. Amen.

Our Father

Our Father, who art in Heaven, hallowed be Thy name; Thy kingdom come; Thy will be done, on earth as it is in Heaven. Give us this day our daily bread, and forgive us our trespasses as we forgive those who trespass against us. And lead us not into temptation, but deliver us from evil. Amen.

Pater noster, qui es in caelis, sanctificétur nomen tuum; advéniat regnum tuum; fiat volúntas tua, sicut in caelo et in terra. Panem nostrum quotidiánum da nobis hódie, et dimítte nobis débita nostra, sicut et nos dimíttimus debitóribus nostris. Et ne nos indúcas in tentatiónem sed líbera nos a malo. Amen.

Hail Mary

Hail Mary, full of grace, the Lord is with thee; blessed are thou among women, and blessed is the fruit of thy womb, Jesus. Holy Mary, Mother of God, pray for us sinners, now and at the hour of our death. Amen.

Ave, María, grátia plena, Dóminus tecum. Benedícta tu in muliéribus, et benedíctus fructus ventris tui, Iesus. Sancta María, Mater Dei, ora pro nobis peccatóribus, nunc et in hora mortis nostrae. Amen.

Glory Be

Glory be to the Father, and to the Son, and to the Holy Spirit; as it was in the beginning, is now, and ever shall be, world without end. Amen.

Glória Patri, et Fílio, et Spíritui Sancto; sicut erat in princípio, et nunc, et semper, et in saecula saeculórum. Amen.

Blessing Before Meals

Bless us, O Lord, and these Thy gifts, which we are about to receive from Thy bounty, through Christ our Lord. Amen.

Benedíc nos Dómine et haec Túa dóna quae de Túa largitáte súmus sumptúri. Per Chrístum Dóminum nóstrum. Amen.

Blessing After Meals

We give thee thanks, almighty God, for all Thy benefits, Who livest and reignest, world without end. Amen.

Ágimus Tíbi grátias, omnípotens Déus, pro univérsis benefíciis Tuis: qui vívis et régnas in saécula saeculórum. Amen.

Other Daily Prayers

By Raymond Leo Cardinal Burke

Prayer to the Sacred Heart

Dear Jesus, with all my heart, with all my soul, with all my mind, and with all my strength, I love You. I beg Your Sacred Heart to forgive those who do not love You with all their heart, with all their soul, with all their mind, and with all their strength. Amen.

Prayer of Reparation to the Sacred Heart

Dear Jesus, with the Immaculate Heart of Mary and the Purest Heart of St. Joseph, I offer all my heart as a gift to Your Sacred Heart so that this small sacrifice may honor You when sins offend You. Amen.

Prayer for the Conversion of Sinners

Dear Jesus, I believe that Your Body, Blood, Soul, and Divinity are truly present in the Most Holy Eucharist. I unite my heart to Your Sacred Heart when I receive You in Holy Communion. And I offer Your Presence in me to the Holy Trinity—You, together with the Father and the Holy Spirit—for the conversion of poor sinners. Amen.

Prayer to Our Lady of Guadalupe

Dear Lady of Guadalupe, your miraculous image on the tilma of St. Juan Diego is so beautiful, so full of signs of God's love for us. The dark ribbon above your womb is a sign that God the Son is incarnate in you. Please intercede with Jesus Unborn for the protection of all unborn children in the womb and for an end of the evil of abortion. Amen.

About the Author and Illustrator

Patrick O'Hearn is a husband and a father. He holds a master's degree in education from Franciscan University. He has authored or co-authored twelve books, including *Parents of the Saints*, *Nursery of Heaven* (co-author), *The Shepherd at the Crib and the Cross*, *Courtship of the Saints*, *The Grief of Dads* (co-author), *Go and Fear Nothing*, *Our Lady of Sorrows*, *The Truth about Hell* (co-author), *Saints Come in All Shapes and Sizes*, *Virtues of the Saints* (co-author), and *The Most Powerful Saints in Exorcisms* (co-author). He is a contributor to Fr. Donald Calloway's book *30 Day Eucharistic Revival*. You can visit his website at patrickrohearn.com.

Adalee Hude is a wife, mom, artist, and Catholic author. She calls her little artistic corner Brightly Hude Studio. Fueled largely by prayer and tea, she has done illustration work for Catholic magazines, prayer journals, stickers, and several Catholic children's books (*Light of Heaven* and *Sanctus, Sanctus, Sanctus*), all for the greater glory of God. Find her work at BrightlyHude.com.

About
Sophia Institute

Sophia Institute is a nonprofit institution that seeks to nurture the spiritual, moral, and cultural life of souls and to spread the Gospel of Christ in conformity with the authentic teachings of the Roman Catholic Church.

Sophia Institute Press fulfills this mission by offering translations, reprints, and new publications that afford readers a rich source of the enduring wisdom of mankind.

Sophia Institute also operates the popular online resource CatholicExchange.com. Catholic Exchange provides world news from a Catholic perspective as well as daily devotionals and articles that will help readers to grow in holiness and live a life consistent with the teachings of the Church.

In 2013, Sophia Institute launched Sophia Institute for Teachers to renew and rebuild Catholic culture through service to Catholic education. With the goal of nurturing the spiritual, moral, and cultural life of souls, and an abiding respect for the role and work of teachers, we strive to provide materials and programs that are at once enlightening to the mind and ennobling to the heart; faithful and complete, as well as useful and practical.

Sophia Institute gratefully recognizes the Solidarity Association for preserving and encouraging the growth of our apostolate over the course of many years. Without their generous and timely support, this book would not be in your hands.

www.SophiaInstitute.com
www.CatholicExchange.com
www.SophiaInstituteforTeachers.org

Sophia Institute Press® is a registered trademark of Sophia Institute.
Sophia Institute is a tax-exempt institution as defined by the Internal Revenue Code, Section 501(c)(3). Tax ID 22-2548708.